The One Minute Secret

The One Minute Secret

Jay A. Parry

Bookcraft
Salt Lake City, Utah

Library of Congress Catalog Card Number: 88-63586
ISBN 0-88494-687-8

First Printing, 1989

Printed in the United States of America

Contents

Acknowledgments   vii

Introduction   ix

The Challenge   1

The First Step   5

The One Minute Secret   13

Putting It to the Test   23

Another Step   29

Finding Focus   39

One Minute for the Family   45

What Would Jesus Do?   63

Sharing the Gift   73

Acknowledgments

It is appropriate to take one minute to thank those who have helped me with this book:

Kenneth Blanchard and Spencer Johnson, who gave me the initial inspiration through their best-selling book *The One Minute Manager;*

My wife, Vicki Parry, who has been supportive and helpful through all my writing projects, who acts as a skillful editor and reader, and who motivates and encourages me in my efforts to grow and improve;

My six children—Trisha, David, Nathaniel, Annaka, Ben, and Elisa—who love me even when I make mistakes, and who are willing to let me learn to be a good father through on-the-job training;

My parents, Atwell and Elaine Parry, who long ago set my feet on the gospel path, and who continue to teach and lift me;

A good friend, Andrew M. Allison, who created the couplet quoted in the last section of this book, and who sets a wonderful example of practicing what he preaches;

Another good friend, Lane Johnson, who willingly reads the things I write, then helps to improve them through his insightful and incisive comments;

A powerful bishop I once had, Jon Reid, who motivated me to read at least a little in the scriptures every single day, and who taught me the blessings that come through asking "What would Jesus do?" at key points in my week;

Those beyond the veil, who make an immeasurable and continuing contribution to who I am and what I can accomplish.

Although all those listed above can fully share in the credit for any good the reader may find in these pages, I alone accept responsibility for any errors.

Introduction

The story in this book is a simple allegory, or parable, about a man who met life's greatest challenge with the One Minute Secret.

He learned what most of us learn sooner or later: When our "things to do" list comes face to face with the time available, the list goes by the way and time marches on.

And then what becomes of our desires to progress and improve?

The answer is to learn to do big things in small amounts of time. An hour is hard to find (or make), and a second is too small to do anything with. But a minute—that's the unit of time that contains the secret.

The careful use of one minute may not make anyone perfect. But the wise combination of our minutes will set a tone, establish a pattern, put our feet on a path.

The One Minute Secret changed the life of the man in this story. It can change yours as well.

The Challenge

Once there was a young elder who was dissatisfied with his life. He had served a mission, married in the temple, accepted Church callings, and served well in them. He held a current temple recommend and visited the temple regularly. He felt his life was basically in order—but he also felt he wasn't progressing as he would like to be.

One evening, after their three children were put in bed, he and his wife sat together to read. But he was restless, and finally he put down his book and began to share his feelings with her.

"I'm just not satisfied with how I'm growing," he said. "When I was on my mission I was learning all the time. I was growing and progressing like never before.

"But now that I'm in the workaday world, it's different. I'm afraid I'm stagnating. And I don't know what to do about it."

She reached over and took his hand. "John, you're one of the best men I've ever known. Honestly. Don't beat yourself over the head because you're not perfect today. Give yourself some time. The Lord gave us a whole lifetime in which to perfect ourselves. He's not going to punish us if we have to use all of it."

John shook his head. "No, Mary, I don't expect immediate perfection. But sometimes I feel that I'm marking time. Why do I go from year to year and always feel inadequate? Why do I set goals and make resolutions and never really achieve what I set out to do?"

He paused and squeezed her hand. "I guess by some standards I'm doing pretty well. But the prophets have promised us over and over again that the Lord has tremendous blessings waiting for us if we will only qualify. Somehow I need to get off this plateau I'm on."

That night after they went to bed, he lay awake for a long time thinking about the nagging feeling inside. *Am I expecting too much of myself?* he wondered. He thought of the rich young man who sought out Jesus during His earthly ministry.

"Master," the young man asked, "what do I need to do to obtain eternal life?"

"Live the commandments," came the answer.

"I've done that ever since I was young. Is there nothing else that I must do?"

"Sell all that you own and give it to the poor."

John thought about the meaning of that scripture. *The Lord isn't requiring all of us to sell all we have and live in poverty. Instead he's asking us to give up the one thing that's keeping us from him. I wonder what's keeping me from being closer to God.*

He finally fell asleep, but he slept restlessly. During the night he dreamed that he was standing before God on the day of final judgment.

"What have you done to qualify to enter the kingdom?" God asked. His voice was soft yet powerful.

"I've kept the commandments," John replied. "I went on a mission, and I married a righteous girl at the right time and in the right place. I attended my meetings and served in the callings the bishop gave to me. I paid my tithing, kept the Word of Wisdom, and tried to observe the Sabbath properly. I did some member missionary work. I did a little genealogical research, though I probably should have done more. I was a good home teacher and rarely missed. I read the scriptures often and said my prayers."

He stopped and waited for a response. It didn't come. He woke up instead. He sat up in the dark and looked out of the window at the sliver of the moon.

"Yes, all those things are needful," he whispered. "But the Lord wants a little more of me. He wants me to constantly progress in my love and my commitment and my closeness to the Spirit. If I stay at the same spiritual level all my life, I'll know only regret and remorse at the end."

Outside, the stars twinkled far above. Despite their distance from the earth, their bright shining seemed warm and comforting.

The First Step

John stewed over his problem for several days. It had grabbed hold of his heart and mind and wouldn't let go.

On Sunday he decided to talk to his elders quorum president about it. President Holden was a true spiritual leader to his quorum. John suspected he had grappled with the same problem before—and had probably come up with some answers.

John pulled him aside just as the quorum meeting was ending. "Matt, I've got a little problem that's bothering me," he said. "Could we get together sometime soon to talk it over?"

"Sure thing," Matt said. "We could meet right after sacrament meeting today if you'd like. Or would you rather do it later?"

"I'd like to do it as soon as possible."

After sacrament meeting had ended they found an empty classroom and shut the door behind them. "If this is a worthiness problem . . . ," Matt began.

"It is," John laughed. "But it's not one for the bishop. Don't worry. I just need some advice." He explained how he had been feeling. "I have a lot of respect for you, Matt. You really seem to be on top of things. And from what I can tell, you get it all done. You're not like most of us. We try to juggle family and employment and Church job and personal improvement, and we end up dropping some of our juggling balls. But you keep them all in the air, perfectly balanced. I'd like to know how you do it."

This time Matt laughed. "You just haven't seen the pile of balls back in my garage! No, John, I'm not nearly as perfect as you seem to think I am." He stopped and looked at the other man for a moment, studying his eyes. "But I do have a few ideas that might be useful to you."

"I'd love to hear them."

"I suppose I should start by telling you how I feel about time. Have you ever thought about how important time is?"

"Sure. I guess better time management would help me some."

"Better time management would help all of us," the president said. "But I'm thinking about time from a little different angle. Time is our lives. It's the very thing our lives are made of. When we run out of time, our lives are over. Maybe that's too obvious to require being said. But bear with me."

He stood and walked over to the chalkboard. He pulled a short stub of chalk out of the pocket of his suit coat. "I always like to keep a piece of chalk handy." He grinned. "Never know when I might need it."

He drew a line on the chalkboard, running from left to right. "Suppose this line represents your life. The line that represents your allotment of time would be exactly the same. So when someone asks what you're going to do with your life, what they really mean is, 'What are you going to do with the time you'll have on this earth?' "

He turned away from the board and looked at John. "By the same token, when you waste some of your time, you're wasting some of your life.

"I believe the Lord is going to hold us accountable for how we use our time in this life. He's going to want to know how we spent our lives—and why we made the choices we did."

John interrupted. "You used the expression 'spent our lives.' It's interesting that we refer to using time and using a part of our lives as *spending.* Time is a valuable commodity, and none of us has an unlimited amount."

"That's exactly right!" Matt smiled and nodded.

Matt continued: "I really like the last part of Rudyard Kipling's poem 'If.' Here's how it goes—but I must admit I've changed the final line." And he recited the words:

If you can fill the unforgiving minute,
With sixty seconds' worth of distance run,
Yours is the earth and everything that's in it,
And, which is more, your greatest challenge will be won.

"That's great," John murmured.

"Now that we're both on the same wavelength," Matt said, "let me give you a basic principle that helps me in my life.

"I used to concentrate on my long-term goals so much that I lost my focus when it came to closer things." He circled the line on the board. "I looked at the entire forest and forgot to look at the individual trees. Maybe that's part of what Jacob had in mind when he talked about 'looking beyond the mark.'

"Most of us do something else that's just as bad: We don't look at the mark at all, or only do it once in a while. We don't really focus on what our life's objectives are and what we need to do to reach them."

He reached up to the line on the board and drew a series of short vertical lines through it. "If we would only break our lives into smaller pieces, we would be able to see the individual trees in the forest better. We'd be able to concentrate on our real goals, not just on getting through each day without going broke or committing a major sin!"

He put the chalk back in his pocket and returned to his seat next to John. "You know how to eat an elephant?"

"I prefer cooked rather than raw," John said.

The president laughed. "Yes, me too. Then, after it's cooked, you eat it a bite at a time.

"It's the same way with our lives. If we break them down into smaller portions we can chew and digest them better. If life is giving you indigestion, maybe you're biting off more than you can chew."

John chuckled, then asked, "So what is this basic principle that helps you in your life?"

"Oh, I didn't tell you." The president stood again and moved to the chalkboard. "It's this." And he wrote on the board, in big letters:

If I want spiritual growth
in my life today,
I must focus *on spiritual growth*
in my mind today.

John read the words, then re-read them. "You're saying that if we want to grow, we've got to make a conscious effort."

"Right. Every day. If you don't think consciously about what you need to do to grow, you'll be going through your life in a haphazard kind of way. You'll stumble along and won't be very effective."

John was intrigued by the thought. "But if I do get that focus in my mind, if I keep a clear view of my spiritual goals and objectives, I'll have more ability to accomplish what I need to."

"More ability, power, commitment, desire. What if you said you wanted to run a marathon in six months and then never thought about that goal again until the time was up? If you truly never thought about it, you wouldn't get out there and train—and when the six months was up, you'd be no more prepared to run the marathon than you were at the beginning."

"That makes sense," John said. "And I guess a lot of us do that spiritually. We say we want to prepare to enter the celestial kingdom; we want to grow to be like God—but we don't focus in on it, and therefore we go a lot of days without training."

"Too many of us miss *most* days, I'm afraid. And you tell me how many training days you can miss if you're really serious about a marathon." Matt paused, looking down. But John could tell he didn't expect an answer. He waited.

Matt continued, "The sad part is this: it's all too easy to drop out of a race when you're not properly trained and conditioned."

Matt stood. "We've got to get home to our families," he said. "But I'll tell you what. You ought to talk to your home teacher about these things. We've had quite a few interviews together, and I think you'll like his insights.''

"I'll do that," John said.

"But let me give you a word of caution right at the outset," Matt said. "We're commanded to improve ourselves. In fact, we're condemned if we don't.

'' 'What manner of men ought ye to be?' Jesus has asked us.

"His answer: 'Verily I say unto you, even as I am.' ''

John interrupted. "That's really the whole focus of the gospel, isn't it. To improve ourselves through repentance and then go out and help others. We become free of sin as He is, filled with faith as He is, powerful in charity as He is."

"Exactly," Matt said. "Now here's the caution I would give you. As you labor to work out your salvation, never forget who makes that salvation possible. Our faith and works are essential, but they mean nothing without the Lord —and we have made covenants to always remember that.

"I have a scripture written in calligraphy and hanging on my bedroom wall to make sure I never forget." He opened his Book of Mormon and read:

> *For we labor diligently to write,*
> *to persuade our children,*
> *and also our brethren,*
> *to believe in Christ,*
> *and to be reconciled to God;*
> *for we know that it is by grace that we are saved,*
> *after all we can do. . . .*
> *And we talk of Christ,*
> *we rejoice in Christ,*
> *we preach of Christ,*

we prophesy of Christ,
and we write according to our prophecies,
that our children may know to what source
they may look for a remission of their sins.
                    —2 Nephi 25:23, 26

"Thank you," John said. "As we struggle to progress, sometimes that's too easy to forget. I guess that's because our personal efforts are so evident, so demanding, sometimes so strenuous. We can't *see* all the things the Lord has done for us. But we can *feel* them if we will only try. I'll be sure to remember."

The One Minute Secret

At home John thought about what President Holden had told him. He shared what he'd learned with Mary.

"The interesting thing," he said, "is that he didn't tell me a single thing I didn't already know. Yet it really hit me. Maybe I was just ready for it. Anyway, I know that unless I get more serious about how I'm spending my life and my time, I'll probably have deep regrets when this life is over."

Their home teachers—an elder and a young priest— stopped by early the next week. They chatted for a few minutes, and the elder asked some subtle questions to learn how the family was doing. The priest gave a short message. At John's request they then joined the family in prayer. As they were walking to the door, John's oldest boy cornered the priest and asked him if he'd seen the Lakers' game the night before. Mary thanked them for coming and went into the next room to help their middle child with a school project. John pulled the senior home teacher aside.

"Phil, I have a quick question for you before you go."

"Okay," Phil said. "Shoot."

"I was talking with Matt Holden the other day about how to really get off the dime and start progressing. He gave me some good ideas, but said I should talk to you."

"Okay," Phil repeated. He stood in thought for a moment, then proceeded.

"Have you noticed how organized Matt is?" Phil asked. "He gets everything done. Rather than being overwhelmed by the complex demands of life, he seems to revel in them."

"If you're around him long you can't miss any of that," John said. "It's fairly clear to me that he has something important going for him."

"That's right," Phil said. "I watched him for a long time before I ever asked him what his secret was. That was before you moved into the ward. At the time he was the deacons quorum advisor and assistant Scoutmaster. One day I approached him, right out of the blue, and told him I wanted to qualify for the celestial kingdom and I was afraid I wasn't going to make it."

"What did he tell you?"

"Well, first he said I was probably doing more things right than I thought I was. Then he said he was glad to know someone who cared enough to make an extra effort." The home teacher paused.

John prodded him. "Then what?"

"Then he gave me this little talk about time. He probably gave the same talk to you."

John smiled and nodded.

"One important idea that helped me immediately was this: If I'm already basically living the commandments I don't need to do a lot more things in my life.

"Many of us are worthy to attend the temple and are praying and reading scriptures and serving in callings and serving in our families. We don't need to discourage ourselves by thinking we have to do a lot of extra things— though we should be open to the Spirit when he tells us things to do.

"Rather than doing a lot of additional things, we need to do better at the things we're already doing. You may not need to say more prayers, for example, but perhaps you need to improve the prayers you're saying."

Phil stopped and looked down at his hands. "That simple idea makes quite a difference in my spiritual life.

"After sharing that concept, Matt told me to go talk to the bishop—said he'd taught him everything he knew. I didn't want to bother the bishop. I was sure he had some people with *real* problems in the ward, and I hesitated to add my own little one. But I did anyway! I really wanted to know what he had to say."

He took a deep breath. "What he said changed my life. He told me this secret—and it's so important that I always carry the words with me." He pulled a card from his pocket and read:

If I can make one minute count,
my life will take care of itself.

"I can be good for one minute," John said.

Phil nodded. "That's what *I* thought."

"But I don't believe one minute can make a saint out of you."

"I thought that too. But what if you pick exactly the right minute?"

"I'm not sure what you mean."

The home teacher looked over at his tall companion and smiled. The young man was standing beside the door, talking about basketball in an animated voice.

"Here's the idea," Phil said. "Suppose you took one minute several times a day and used it to focus in on your true objectives. What do you think would happen in your life?"

"I don't know. One minute doesn't seem to be much time."

"Let me get more specific. Pardon me if I get personal here, but you asked for it. I imagine you offer a private prayer every day, right?"

"Yes," John said.

"Do you read the scriptures regularly?"

"Most days."

"Let me take just those two things as examples," Phil said. "You're already reading the scriptures pretty faithfully, and you're praying. Those things help you to stay close to the Spirit.

"But what if you could do something to make your prayers more meaningful? What if you did something to let the scriptures sink more deeply into your heart?"

John was getting more and more intrigued. He motioned for his home teacher to sit down on the couch, then sat down beside him. "What would do those things for me?"

"That's the One Minute Secret!" Phil said. "Try it and you'll see that it really does help. *Spend just one minute every day, right before you pray, and think about what you want to talk to our Heavenly Father about.* You may even want to write a few thoughts down. Meditate on your blessings and seek to obtain the presence of the Spirit."

"I can see how that could make a difference," John said. "Even one minute's preparation is more than I've been spending. I must admit that I kind of jump into my prayers without a whole lot of thought." He pulled a notebook from his pocket and wrote the idea down in it:

Before I pray each day,
I will spend one minute
to consider what I need to pray about.
I will seek God's Spirit.

He looked back up from his notebook. "But what if I can't think of anything in that one minute?"

"There's nothing sacred about one minute!" the home teacher exclaimed. "Take five minutes if you want to. The choice is yours. Once you get started you'll find yourself growing and progressing in measurable ways, and you'll be happy to take several minutes instead of one.

"On the other hand, we can do a lot more in one minute than we think we can. It's just that most of us have never tried it."

"I guess I should try it, shouldn't I," John said.

"Let me offer another suggestion while I'm at it," Phil said. "At one point I was concerned that all my prayers were getting to be the same. I know now I just wasn't putting enough thought and energy into them.

"I decided to do a careful survey of what the scriptures say about praying. I learned that I should make a practice of praying out loud, for instance. The scriptures repeatedly tell us to lift our voices to the heavens when we pray. That meant I needed to find a private place—the scriptures call it a secret place or a closet—so I could concentrate and speak without any fear of being overheard or interrupted.

"I also learned that I should reach outside of myself in my prayers, to consistently be concerned about others.

"I think combining those practices with the One Minute Secret helped me a great deal as I tried to establish a meaningful communication with my Heavenly Father."

"That's going to help me," John said. "I can tell already. Not too long ago I read in one of the Church magazines about a lady who really reached out to others in her prayers. Every morning she'd kneel and ask, 'Who needs me today?' Invariably she'd get a feeling about someone specific she knew—one of her children, a neighbor, a relative."

"I remember reading that too," Phil said. "It changed her life."

"So why did I just read it without trying it?" John said. He didn't expect an answer. He glanced at his watch. "I know I've kept you, but do you have time to tell me about using the One Minute Secret with the scriptures?"

Phil looked at his own watch and shook his head. "I'm afraid I'd better get to my next appointment. They expected us ten minutes ago. But I'll come back whenever you'd like, and we can talk some more."

"How about tomorrow night?"

"Sure. I've got to go to a meeting at the church tomorrow and I can stop by afterwards—about nine, I would guess."

Putting It to the Test

Later that night, when the house was quiet, John went into the little room he and Mary shared as a combination office/sewing room. He sat at his desk and pulled a blank sheet of paper from one of the drawers.

To be more effective in my prayers, he thought, *I've got to focus in on what I need to be praying about.*

He thought about his usual approach to prayer: when the time for prayer came he would kneel on the floor, thank Heavenly Father for some of his blessings, and ask for help with some of the problems that were bothering him. He usually finished up in a couple of minutes or so—and he usually stood back up without having felt anything special.

"That's got to change," he whispered. "I'm going to be talking with God, my Father, the Being who created me. If I open up a true communication, I'll feel the Spirit with me while I pray." He thought for a moment. "If I don't feel the Spirit, I first need to make sure my heart and hands are pure. Then I need to persist until I succeed."

A thought occurred to him then, and he wrote it in bold letters on his paper:

Three steps to effective prayer: Prepare, prepare, prepare.

And that's why the One Minute Secret works with prayer, he thought. *It gets me to prepare before I start.*

He sat for a moment and stared at the paper before him. It felt a little funny to be taking notes on a prayer he was going to offer.

But then he realized that it felt funny only because he had never done it before.

He remembered that when President David O. McKay asked the General Authorities to write out their general conference addresses in advance, one said that he preferred to speak as the Spirit dictated when he was standing at the pulpit.

President McKay responded that the Spirit could dictate just as effectively a week in advance, or two weeks, or a month.

John whispered a prayer in his heart, asking to be guided in the things he wrote down, asking to be directed by the Spirit. Then he began to write. At the top of the sheet he put two headings:

| TO THANK FOR | TO ASK FOR |

Under the first heading he wrote—
    home
    family
    good job
    modern conveniences
    health

He looked at the list for a moment, then scratched it out. "Got to get more specific," he muttered.

He recalled a tip a writing teacher had given him once. "Focus up close," she'd said. "If you have a dog in your story, don't just have it be a dog. Make it a specific dog—a Doberman or a poodle. That will bring life to your story."

The same principle, John realized, would also help bring life to his prayers. He needed to focus up close on the things he needed to pray about. He tried again:
    Mary, with her patience and humor
    Mary's commitment to the gospel and her desire to share spiritual things
    Three children who love me unconditionally and make me feel like a million bucks—Tom, Jeffrey, and Suzanne
    Employment that is fulfilling and rewarding—I was so blessed to get this job in the first place, and it's getting better all the time
    My knowledge that God lives and that he loves and cares about me
    My knowledge of the plan of salvation, with all the blessings that brings into my life

He stared at the list for a moment, then turned to the second column and wrote:

The thing I'm most concerned about right now is my spiritual state—I need help

Jeffrey is having real struggles with math at school

He thought what Phil had said about reaching outside himself. He wrote:

Our prophet is getting old—needs support

Missionary effort

Our neighbors, the Millers—we've got to find a way to share the gospel with them

Sister Steadman—her cancer treatments are really making her weak

When he had finished writing his notes, he glanced at the clock. It had taken him only a few minutes, but he felt even that effort was going to help. He knew he usually wouldn't take notes in advance. But this time it had helped get him onto the right track.

He pushed back the chair and knelt on the cold tile floor. He closed his eyes and began to pour his heart out in prayer, speaking first about his deep desire to be a better person, to be closer to the Spirit, to be more worthy of his rich blessings and of those he hoped eventually to receive.

It wasn't necessary, he found, to open his eyes to refer to his paper. His preparation had put his mind into gear, and the thoughts flowed. He knew the Spirit was present.

When he had said all that was in his heart, he began to close the prayer. Then he stopped. It had been all monologue thus far. He had learned long before that true prayer is a dialogue, a two-way communication—even though he did not often apply the idea. This time he remained on his knees, listening for whisperings from the Spirit.

What he heard was disconcerting: "John, I'm pleased that you desire these blessings for yourself and others. Now go forth and find ways in which you can help to bring these things to pass."

John got up off his knees and looked at the paper. He picked up his pencil and made some additional notations, writing down the things the Spirit put into his heart:

1. Continue to search and work on own spirituality. Keep applying what I'm learning, and seek to learn more from Phil and others.

2. Spend some time teaching Jeffrey the basic techniques of multiplication and division.

3. Bear testimony about our prophet in our next testimony meeting. Remind others to join in exercising faith in his behalf.

4. Talk to Mary about budget. Can we give a little toward missionary fund each month?

5. Visit the Millers Saturday. Excuse: ask what he does with his melons to get them to grow in this climate.

6. Go with Mary to visit Sister Steadman before our dinner date this Friday. See if we should take some food in to her.

He looked at the list and smiled to himself. He had a warm feeling inside. He had put forth just a little more effort in prayer, and the Lord had spoken to him.

It was late, and John knew he should be getting to bed. But before he went he took a minute to summarize what he had learned about the One Minute Secret:

Applying the One Minute Secret to Prayer— A Summary

1. Realize that if I can make some of my little minutes count, my whole life will be more focused and will go much better. I will be much more able to reach my eternal goals.
2. Prepare for prayer by thinking about the communication before I begin. Remember that I'll be talking to the most important and powerful Being in the universe. I should take pains to get my thoughts in order before I start.
3. Seek to pray in the Spirit. I will pray most efficaciously when I let Heavenly Father help me know what to pray for and about.
4. Before I close the prayer, take a few moments to listen to the Spirit. The purpose of prayer is not just to pour my heart out to my Heavenly Father, but also to receive into my heart messages he wishes to send me.
5. After the prayer is over, write down what I've felt and what I've learned. Write down what I'm going to do now.
6. Go forth and do it!

Another Step

Phil rang the bell at five minutes to nine the next night. Mary opened the door and invited him in. John was sitting on the couch with his Book of Mormon open on his lap. He gestured for Phil to sit beside him. Mary sat on John's other side.

"I'm glad you could come," John said. "I told Mary what we talked about last night, and she bawled me out for not including her."

"Good for you!" Phil laughed, looking at Mary. Then he said, more seriously, "I was hoping I could see you both tonight. I think you'll have more success with the One Minute Secret if you work on it together."

He shifted on the couch to make himself more comfortable. "Now, where were we?"

John gestured toward the Book of Mormon. "You were going to tell us how to apply the One Minute Secret to our scripture reading."

"Great!" Phil said. "I truly love the scriptures. The prophets have told us over and over again that we should read the scriptures every day. I believe that can make a big difference in how we feel about life and about ourselves.

"I once had a bishop who really pushed this. He said we should open the scriptures *every single day of our lives* and read at least one word. I started doing that. Of course, I never stopped with just one word. I at least had to finish the verse. And usually I read on and finished the page or the chapter.

"But having that minimum goal of one word per day really helped. I went from a pattern of hit-and-miss to one of never missing a day.

"It wasn't hard to make the switch. All I had to do was find a goal I could handle and then make sure I focused in on it every day."

He leaned forward and flipped open his own Book of Mormon. "So we were going to talk about the One Minute Secret as it applies to reading the scriptures. Say you've decided you're going to read at least something in the scriptures every day. That's a wonderful start. But you need to take it a step farther if you truly want to benefit.

"You know the difference between saying words in prayer and really communicating with our Father in Heaven. You need to make the same leap when you approach the scriptures. It's good to read them. It's even better to study them. Best of all is to hunger and thirst for the word so much that you do what Nephi said we ought to do: 'Feast on the words of Christ.' "

"I've had that experience from time to time," John said. "It's not something you forget."

Phil smiled. "That's for sure." He flipped a few pages until he settled on Mosiah 5. "Here's a good scripture to illustrate what I'm talking about. First we'll read verse seven. This is King Benjamin speaking:

" 'And now, because of the covenant which ye have made ye shall be called the children of Christ, his sons, and his daughters; for behold, this day he hath spiritually begotten you; for ye say that your hearts are changed through faith on his name; therefore, ye are born of him and have become his sons and his daughters.' "

"That's always been a favorite of mine," Mary said.

"Yes," Phil agreed. "There's a lot of power packed into just a few words in that verse.

"Now, here's how to use the One Minute Secret with the scriptures. Let me write it down for you." He took a sheet of notepaper and wrote:

> *After you read the scriptures each day,*
> *take one minute and ponder them.*
> *Ask questions.*
> *Liken them to yourself.*
> *Find the meaning for you in your life today.*

"I usually keep my notebook handy to write down insights and things I need to do with what I've read. But for now I'll just think out loud to give you an idea of what I like to do."

He looked down at the opened Book of Mormon and began to read and speak softly.

"Because of the covenant which ye have made . . .

"I've made the same covenant as the Nephites did—to look to the Lord and follow him and trust in him.

"Ye shall be called the children of Christ . . .

"How does a child behave? He'll often follow the parent. He'll have many of the same characteristics as the parent. Have I developed the characteristics of the Lord in my life?

"We've been commanded to honor our parents. Do I honor the Lord, as the one who has given birth to my new spiritual life? Can another person tell by my actions that I really have been *spiritually begotten* by the Lord? Am I true to my new parentage? What do I need to do better?

"If I examine my obedience I can see that I need to improve my efforts in sharing the gospel with others. I need to get rid of a couple of things in my observance of the Sabbath that hinder me in truly worshipping God that day. I need to spend more time and better time with my wife and children. I'll write down some specific plans to put these resolves into practice.

"Your hearts are changed through faith on his name . . .

"I've felt that my heart has been changed. I'd be a different person if I didn't know about the Lord and his atonement and the power he exercises in my life. But do I consistently act as this different person, this person with a changed heart? Or do I forget my new life and slip back into old habits and old negative patterns?

"Tonight when I pray I'll need to ask my Heavenly Father to help me to understand myself better, to reveal my true heart to me, to help me to be aware of things in my life that are subtly holding me back."

He looked back over at John and Mary. "That will give you an idea of how I do it. Of course, I'm not so inhibited when I'm alone as when I'm with someone else, even a good friend."

"I really like this idea," John said. He made a note of it:

*Don't just read the scriptures, but feast.
Ponder!*

He looked at his note for a moment, then added with a flourish:

Let the solemnities
of the eternities
sink deep into my heart.

Then he turned back to Phil. "I like this idea, and I think it would usually help. But you've got to admit that you specially selected a verse that lends itself to the One Minute Secret. What do you do when the verse doesn't mean that much to you—like the long, long sections of wars in the book of Alma?"

"If the verse you've read doesn't speak to your spirit," Phil answered, "I think you'd better read another, and another, until you find one that does hit you.

"But I believe every single page in the scriptures has something important for us today. I'll flip completely at random to a page in the 'war section' of Alma and we'll see what to do with it."

He turned back in the book until he reached Alma 43, then quickly flipped a few more pages over.

"Okay, take a look here at the bottom of page 328, verse seven. It says here that 'Amalickiah had . . . been obtaining power by fraud and deceit,' but that Moroni 'had been preparing the minds of the people to be faithful unto the Lord their God.'

"If I were to spend one minute pondering this verse, I think I'd start to get some insights I wouldn't get if I were just reading it through.

"One thing that comes to mind is the different approaches to success in life, Satan's path and the Lord's path. Both are evident in this one verse.

"Satan teaches people to grab wealth or power or anything else using whatever means will work. The ends justify the means, he says.

"Do you want power? It can be yours! Smear the name of your opponent, and people will reject him and turn to you. Stab him in the back, tell lies, destroy his reputation, and you will emerge the victor.

"If you're desperate enough, you can remove your opponent through murder, as Cain did, as Saul tried to do with David, as Laman and Lemuel tried to do with Nephi, as Amalickiah did with the Lamanite king. Then you can take his place as the favored one.

"Of course, we see this insidious approach to power in our own day. You don't have to murder to use fraud and deceit. All you have to do is lead others to conclusions that aren't quite true, to falsely place yourself in a better light than your rival, advancing yourself by tearing him down."

He glanced up at John and Mary, then looked back down at the book. "Then we have the other side of it, shown in Moroni's approach. While Amalickiah was 'obtaining power by fraud and deceit,' Moroni was helping his people 'to be faithful unto the Lord their God.'

"Moroni was interested in another kind of power: spiritual power, which comes through faithfulness. Ultimately that's the only kind of power there is, because our temporal, earthly successes will pass away, but spiritual power can be ours forever, if we endure to the end.

"And what can be the effect of this spiritual power? The Lord has given us promise after promise, saying that if we'll only be faithful he will cleanse us and heal us and make us whole, he will bless us with the companionship of the Holy Ghost, he will help our testimonies to grow. And, as Moroni knew, if we are faithful and doing God's will, he will help us fight our battles.

"I'm very impressed with the contrast between Amalickiah's approach to life and Moroni's approach. And I can't help but ask myself: What is my approach? Do I seek to gain power and success in this life through illegitimate means? Am I unconsciously following Satan's path? Or am I on the path of faithfulness, trying to gain spiritual power by walking on the Lord's path?

"Look now at the next verse. I see there an important addendum to Moroni's preparation effort with his people. He did not simply tell them to trust in the Lord. He also worked tirelessly to prepare their cities physically—building forts, 'throwing up banks of earth,' and erecting walls of stone to protect their land from the invading Lamanites. He knew that while we must rely on the Lord to help us in this life, we must also do everything in our power to help ourselves."

Phil flipped over a few pages again at random, then jabbed his finger at the bottom of page 336.

"I see here at the bottom of the page that it says a certain group of the Nephites wanted to have kings instead of judges. 'Now those who were in favor of kings were those of high birth, . . . and they were supported by those who sought power and authority over the people.'

"That would get me pondering over the problems of pride and love of power and authority. That's easy for us to apply to ourselves. Even the best of us, I'm afraid, has at least a little challenge with those temptations."

"Not me!" John exclaimed. "The only thing I'm proud of is that I'm so humble!"

They all laughed. Mary added, "And I'm humbled that I'm married to a man who is proud of only one thing!" They laughed again.

Then Phil said, "Can you see how easy it is to find material in the scriptures that applies to you with your problems of today? If you don't find it in the first verse you read, read on for a few more.

"What we need to do, with the help of the Holy Ghost, is create our own personal commentary on the scriptures. It doesn't have to be fancy or formal. No one else need ever see it. One friend of mine scratches notes in every white space he can find in his scriptures. Those scriptures are a wonder to behold! But they mean a lot more to him than they did before he started making his notes.

"I've found that until I can bring the scriptures into my own life, I don't enjoy a fraction of the power they could bring to me."

Mary nodded and said: "I read once that it helps sometimes to put your own name into the scriptures when you read them. For example, we were talking about humility a minute ago. Doctrine and Covenants 112:10 is a wonderful scripture about that—but it really starts to come alive for me when I put my own name into it: 'Be thou humble, *Mary*; and the Lord thy God shall lead thee by the hand, and give thee answer to thy prayers.' "

"I like that," Phil said. "You're hitting on a valuable key to spiritual growth." And he reached for the notepaper and wrote the words as he said them:

> ***I will grow just as much
> as I make a conscious effort
> to make the gospel active
> in my life.***

They talked for a while longer; then Phil had to go. While the ideas were fresh in their minds, John and Mary consulted their notes and compiled a summary of what they had learned:

Applying the One Minute Secret to Scripture Reading—A Summary

1. I will make a commitment to read the scriptures every day, even if only a tiny portion.
2. After I read the scriptures, I will take one minute and ponder what I've read. I will ask questions and liken the scriptures to myself. I will write down my insights and the things I need to do.
3. I will make an effort to apply the scriptures to myself directly. Unless I personalize what I read, I'm doing little more than reviewing words in a book.
4. I will remember that I will grow precisely to the extent that I make a conscious effort to make the gospel active in my life.

Finding Focus

The morning was quiet. John awoke early, stretched, and sat up in bed. Mary sighed in her sleep and turned her head on her pillow without waking.

It's going to be a great day, John thought. *I can feel it in my bones.*

Several weeks had passed since his conversations with Phil. The time had been well spent. Almost every day he had consciously applied the ideas he had learned.

Before he prayed he spent at least one minute getting himself into the proper spirit and thinking about some of the things he wanted to pray about.

During his prayer he spent some time listening to the whisperings of the Spirit, receiving feelings and impressions about the things he'd been mentioning in his prayer.

After praying he took a moment and wrote those impressions down.

He made a special effort to read the scriptures every day. He was pleased that he hadn't missed a single day since he made that commitment.

After he read, he took at least one minute to ponder the word of the Lord.

The results of his efforts had taken him by surprise. He was amazed to see what significant benefits could come from small efforts.

He moved to the edge of the bed and put his feet on the floor. Mary's eyes fluttered and opened.

"Good morning," he said. "Did you have a good rest?"

She smiled sleepily and nodded.

"I'm glad you're awake," he said. "I've been thinking about the One Minute Secret and I wanted to talk to you. I'm thinking that the main thing that was missing from my life before was the daily focus. That's such a simple thing, but it makes a genuine difference."

She nodded her head in agreement. "I've been having some of the same thoughts," she said.

"That's why the One Minute Secret opens doors for me. It forces me to take a minute several times a day to look at things from an eternal perspective."

He shifted on the side of the bed, bringing one leg up and sitting on it. "When I go through day after day without really looking inward, I end up simply going through the motions. I say prayers, I read scriptures, I hold family home evenings—but I'm so busy making a living and trying to cope with family problems and taking care of the mechanics of my Church job that I don't take the time to see where I am and why I'm doing what I'm doing.

"But when I take one minute at key points during the day and use it to reestablish in my mind and heart why I'm here and what I'm supposed to emphasize in my life, it takes my actions and moves them from the mundane to the sublime."

He smiled. "It even makes me poetic!"

Mary sat up, puffed up her pillow behind her, and leaned back on it. "When I was in high school," she said, "I got a nice camera for Christmas one year. It was a 35-millimeter. It had ways to adjust for the amount of light and the length of exposure and the distance between me and what I was photographing.

"I went through a lot of rolls of film before I really learned how to use it properly. But my father was patient and kept buying me new rolls and paying to develop the old ones.

"As I think about it now, learning to use that camera was much like learning to develop my spirit.

"If I didn't have enough light, my picture would be black. If I had too much light, the picture would come out all white."

"The light of Christ to our spirits," John said quietly.

"Yes. The Lord gives the light of Christ to all of us. Everyone on earth has light to work with, and if they live right they can receive even more light. But not too much too soon—the Lord knows that could harm us."

"I see where you're going," John said. "Light plus focus equals good pictures—and eternal life. Right?"

Mary leaned forward. "You must be a professional photographer," she teased. "Or something."

"Well, I am something."

Mary laughed, then continued: "You're right that one trick of using the camera was learning how to focus. If I focused too close in or too far away, my picture would be fuzzy. I couldn't see clearly what I'd photographed.

"And what happens when we fail to find focus for our lives? We wander around and make little progress from day to day. When we don't take time to focus in on the important things, we end up without ever seeing clearly where we are or what we should be doing."

"Some people never even take the cap off their lens," John said.

"That's true, isn't it." She sat silent for a moment, looking thoughtful. Then she said, "I'm just grateful our Father is patient with us while we learn."

John reached across the bed and gave her a long hug.

Later in the day he found a new sign posted on the refrigerator:

If we want to progress,
we must see clearly where we are
and where we are going.
If we want to see clearly,
we must focus.

One Minute for the Family

Only a couple of days went by before Mary pulled John aside one evening with a serious look on her face. "We've got to have a little talk," she said.

"I was just on my way down to the office to do some work," he protested.

"Your work can wait," she said. "But our talk can't."

John could tell she meant what she said. He nodded. "I think you're right," he said.

They went to their bedroom and closed the door. John leaned against the wall. Mary sat on the edge of the bed. "We've got a problem with the kids, and it's getting worse. We've got to do something now."

John frowned. "What's the matter? Things seem to be going pretty well."

"You're so busy you don't see everything that goes on around here. Let me tell you." She folded her arms and looked him squarely in the face.

"First of all, Tom is getting a pretty rotten attitude about helping around the house. You know how he used to be my wonderful little helper. Now it's a constant battle just to get him to pick up his clothes. I've threatened and bribed and cajoled and yelled. I'm at my rope's end. I just don't know what to do."

"I knew he was giving you a little trouble," John said. "But I had no idea it was this bad."

"Then there's Jeffrey. He's still struggling with math at school. For some reason he can't quite get the idea.

"But that's not the worst of it. What I'm worried about is what it's doing to his self-image. You know how he used to be so good at reading and spelling. Well, now he's starting to think he can't even do that. I think he's taken one step forward and three steps back this year.

"Since Suzanne is still so little, her problems are on a different level. But they're certainly real to her. She needs more time with both of us. She needs to be hugged and read to and rocked in the rocking chair. She needs someone to talk to her at the end of her day, when it's time for her to go to bed. She needs a bedtime story and song.

"I'm giving her a lot of that. But I'll be honest with you, John. You're so busy with everything—your work, your Church job, this house that's always needing repairs, your efforts to improve yourself—that I think you're forgetting your family."

Mary's voice was gentle, but the words stung. John had been pleased with the progress he had been making. But now he realized that he still didn't have balance in his life. He was trying to grow and progress in one area while ignoring the needs of the most important individuals in his life.

His first impulse was to defend himself. He was already stretched thin. He loved his children and did what he could for them. What right did she have to demand more?

But he swallowed his pride. "I'm not sure what to do," he said. "I agree with what you're saying, but what can I do about it? You know my schedule."

"I've thought about that," Mary said. She reached over and pulled him down to sit next to her. "If you could just spend a few minutes a day with each child it would make a difference. You're the head of our home. You have the priesthood. If you would just take the time to reach out to them you'd discover how to help."

John was silent for a moment. Then a bright new insight began to form in his mind. "You know what I could do?" His voice was filled with excitement. "I don't know why I didn't think of this before. I could apply the One Minute Secret to the needs of my family."

Mary smiled. "I've wondered if there might be an application there."

He pondered for a moment longer, then said, "One thing I could do is make sure each child knows he or she is important and valued to me." He walked around the end of the bed and went to his nightstand. He returned with his notebook and a pencil. "I've got to write this down. This could really help."

To teach my family how important they are to me:
Take one minute each day,
Give each person a hug,
Say "I love you."

"That's a great place to start," Mary said. Then she added, slyly, "I hope you're including me when you make these resolutions."

John abruptly sat beside her and pulled her close in a tight hug. "Of course," he whispered. "You come first. And I love you."

He held her for a few minutes. They hugged without speaking. Then he stood again. "I know that one-minute hugging idea will help with our children, and it's got to help our relationship too. But that's only the beginning point. I wonder what else I could do."

"How about this," Mary said. "Like I said, I've been thinking.

"What if you took some time each day to really be with each child. Talk about what they want to talk about, and look into their eyes when you do it. Listen and respond. I believe that would do wonders for your relationship with them. And it would help them to feel better about themselves."

"Yes!" John almost shouted it. He pulled his notebook from his shirt pocket and wrote in it, saying the words aloud as he wrote:

At least once each day,
I'll give each family member
my undivided attention.
For a few moments each day,
I will totally belong to the person I am with.

"I was hoping you would come up with something like this," Mary said. "But what are you going to do about your time problem? Where are you going to find time to be with three kids separately every day?"

"And with a wife, who deserves all the kids get and more." John stared at the floor for a moment. When he looked back up he was halfway frowning. "You're right that I need to be giving more to the family. That should be my first priority, along with developing myself. I guess I've been neglecting all of you.

"If it is so very important to build my relationship with my wife, and to love and teach my children, should I let other things steal my time away from you all?" He didn't wait for an answer, but rushed on.

"That's my first thought.

"But my second thought is of the One Minute Secret. It will take more than one minute to strengthen my ties with my family, of course, but if I can spend a minute really being with each person, it will give me a marvelous start."

Mary nodded. "For me, the hardest part of being with the children, really being with them, is just pulling myself away from whatever I'm doing and deciding to give them some time."

"Mc too," John said. "That's why the One Minute Secret will work here. It will get me with them. And with you. Then, once I've made the move to spend time with someone in the family, I'll be able to let my heart take the lead."

"A journey of a thousand miles begins with the first step," Mary said.

"Yes," John answered. "And a fulfilling experience with my family begins with the first minute."

The next evening, after supper and family prayer, John decided to go downstairs to his office. He had quite a bit of work he'd brought home from the office, and one of his projects had a tight deadline. Tom was working on his homework in front of the TV, while Jeffrey was just watching it. Suzanne was hanging onto her mother's leg, whining.

John gave Mary a quick hug as he passed through the kitchen. "I've got a big project I've got to work on, hon," he said. "I'll try not to be down there too long."

Mary gave him a disappointed look and glanced down at Suzanne. John shrugged and went down the stairs.

But he began to have second thoughts before he even got through the office door. *I need to spend a little time with the kids tonight,* he thought. *I can get to work after they're in bed.*

He turned back around, climbed the stairs, and went back into the kitchen. Mary's face brightened. He picked up Suzanne and held her close.

"How about a story, Suzy?" he asked.

"I want to read *Christina Katerina and the Box,*" she said.

"I like that story," John said.

They found a quiet corner and sat down together. John opened the book and began to read. It felt good to be there with his little daughter, spending some time just with her. She snuggled next to him and made him feel like the most important person in the world.

After he had helped her say her prayer and tucked her into bed, he went into the living room. Tom and Jeffrey were still sitting in front of the television set, although Tom had dropped all semblance of doing homework. "What's up, boys?" John asked.

"Nothing much," Tom said. He didn't move his eyes from the television screen.

"What are you watching?"

"Some new comedy," Tom said. "It's pretty good."

John looked at his watch. The show would be over in only five minutes. He sat on the couch between the two boys and enjoyed the conclusion of the show with them. Then he said, "It's almost time for bed. But before you go I want to spend a little time with both of you."

"What did we do?" Jeff asked.

"Nothing," John answered. "I just want to be with you."

He went with Jeff into his bedroom. "How are you doing on your Cub Scouts?" he asked.

"I've got most of my requirements for my Bear," Jeff answered. "But there are a few I need some help on."

"Let's work on some for a bit," John said.

Jeff found his book under his bed and opened it to the section about tall tales. "I want to do this achievement," he said. "Will you help me learn more about some of these stories?"

They sat together on the floor, with their backs against the wall, and looked at the book. It gave brief synopses of the stories of Paul Bunyan, Pecos Bill, Rip Van Winkle, Johnny Appleseed and others. Jeff read aloud what each story was about. Then John told some of the details he remembered from the stories.

When they were finished, he watched Jeff play the Folklore Match Game in the book, matching legendary figures with key elements from their stories.

"Can we do this again tomorrow?" Jeff asked when they were finished. "I like it when you help me."

John gave him a hug, waited while he said his prayer, then tucked him into bed. When he went back into the living room, Mary was talking to Tom.

"We're just spending a little time together," Mary said. "I haven't seen much of Tom today."

"Well, I don't want to bother you," John said. "Maybe I should—"

Mary shook her head. "No, we've had a nice talk. We were just finishing up."

"Can we play a game of checkers before I go to bed?" Tom asked.

"Sure." John smiled. "Remember, I said I wanted to spend some time with you. Now it's your turn."

After they'd played three games of checkers, having a pleasant conversation as they played, Tom went to his room to bed. John found Mary sitting on their own bed, her back propped with pillows, reading a book.

"How did it go?" she asked.

"Great!" he said. "Why didn't I start this sooner?"

"Maybe you're like the rest of us," she said with a smile. "Maybe you just didn't think of it."

He grinned back. "You're right, of course." He sat next to her on the bed. "And now it's your turn. Truly the first shall be the last—but not the least. Do you have a minute to talk?"

"What do you think?" Mary asked. "I've been dying to share the insights I've been getting from this book. So make yourself comfortable!"

John and Mary talked for a few minutes, then they knelt together for their evening prayer. John felt warm inside. *Spending time with my family was one of the most impor-*

tant things I've done all day, he thought. He gave Mary a hug and kiss and told her he loved her.

Finally he went down to his office. He had spent just over an hour with Mary and his children, and he knew he'd have to stay up an hour later to make up for it. But he felt good about his decision. Each child had gone to bed feeling loved and feeling important. He and Mary had parted feeling a little closer. That was definitely worth an hour of his time.

John knew he wouldn't be able to spend that kind of individual time with Mary or his children every night. Some evenings he had to go to meetings. Once a week he went on a date with Mary. Monday nights were filled with family home evening.

But if I can give myself that one-minute start every night that I honestly can, I'll be doing great things for my family, he thought. *And for myself.*

John grew increasingly enthusiastic about his new approach with his children. "I like what I'm seeing in the kids," he said to Mary. "But I think they'd do even better if you were to renew your own efforts with them."

She agreed. She was with the children most of the day, except when they were in school—but it wasn't often she gave any of them her undivided attention.

"I'll do better," she said. "What's good for the gander should be good for the goose, right?"

It didn't take long for them to see the results of their new commitment. As they each spent a little time with each of their children several nights a week, John and Mary soon noticed a change in the children's attitudes. They were measurably happier. They seemed to have a better sense of self-esteem. They were more cooperative. They whined less and fought less.

It was rewarding for John to consider what a little extra time with his children had brought.

And he could tell that they looked forward to their one-on-one time with their dad. Each one began to plan in advance how he or she would spend the private time with Daddy.

Unfortunately, as John put it to Mary, even with their improvement the kids were "still far less than little angels."

Sometimes Tom was rude to Jeffrey—and Jeff responded by hitting Tom. Tom reacted in kind, hitting back.

Sometimes Jeff teased Suzanne until she cried and went running to tattle.

Sometimes all three children got going in a quickly deteriorating round of fighting, complete with yelling, hitting, and crying.

John was disturbed by such unhappy times in their home. He knew that a certain amount of bickering and quarreling was normal in a home with children. He remembered how he and his brothers had fought. Sometimes they had been stopped only by their mother yelling at them and punctuating her words with the sting of a willow across their backsides.

But as much as he was upset by his children's behavior at such times, he was even more upset with himself. He had little patience with their hitting and fighting. Whenever he caught one of his children misbehaving, he judged quickly and harshly. He yelled and spanked.

When the kids got their loudest, he yelled that it wasn't good to yell.

When they hit each other, he swatted them on the rear to teach them not to hit.

He was happy to see the improvement in their behavior after he began spending time with them. But they weren't perfect little angels yet. And his approach to discipline wasn't helping.

He talked the problem over with Mary. "Some days they do well. Other days they seem to go on a rampage."

He shook his head and frowned. "I'm afraid those are the days I go on a rampage as well."

"I'm as guilty as you are," Mary said. "And then I feel horrible about it afterward."

"We've been progressing in some areas of our lives," John said. "I don't want this problem to hold us back. Or our children. Let's find something that will help us do better."

They stewed over it for several days. They studied and pondered and prayed.

One morning John came out of the bathroom with his face lathered up and half shaved. "I think I have an answer," he exclaimed. "It won't solve all our problems, but I think it will help."

Mary was brushing her hair in front of the bedroom mirror. "An answer to what?" she asked.

"Our problem with the kids."

"Oh? I want to hear it." She put down the brush and turned to him, giving him her full attention.

"It's as simple as the One Minute Secret," John said. "Whenever we have trouble with the children, before we go barging in with reprisals and punishments and solutions, we should take a minute to regain our perspective.

"I believe most of my trouble with the children comes when I react to them without remembering who they are."

"Who they *really* are," Mary added. "I see what you mean. I recently read a good statement on this and clipped it out. It's in the kitchen. We should make a big poster of it and hang it on the wall." She quickly found the clipping, which read:

Remember:
Each of your children
is a beloved child of God.
He has eternal goals for each of them,
and so do you.

"That's just what I was thinking," John said. He moved over to the dresser and leaned back against it.

"We've both read some of the popular child-rearing books, and we've found some helpful ideas in them. And I think we both have some good instinctive ways to deal with the children when they misbehave—if we could only stop letting our anger and frustration get in the way."

"Yes, we know better when we choose wrong. So how do we use the One Minute Secret to regain perspective and *do* better?" Mary asked.

"I think this will help," John said. "Whenever there is conflict in the home, or whenever we can tell conflict is brewing, we should take one minute and remember who the offending child really is, from an eternal view. We can then offer a brief prayer, asking for help to act accordingly.

"If we will listen to the Spirit and let our better selves prevail—and if we will react the way we really know we should—I think we'll find ourselves building the children up rather than tearing them down."

Mary moved closer to John and slipped her arm around his waist. "I heard a story once that fits with what you're saying," she said.

"Long, long ago there was a rich sultan who had three wives in three different palaces. He had children by all three wives, and he loved his large family dearly.

"War came to his country, and he was forced to go off to battle. The weeks dragged on to months and the months to years. He yearned to be with his family. He longed once again to hold his wives close and to hold his children on his knee.

"Finally a truce was declared and the sultan returned home. His family received him with joy and thanksgiving.

"But immediately he could tell all was not right.

"The children of his first wife treated him with love and

respect—but the second group of children were disdainful, and the third group were sullen.

"He wondered how this could be. In the weeks that followed his homecoming, he watched his three wives carefully.

"The second wife let her children do whatever they wished. If they asked for something they invariably received it. 'I love my children so much I can't say no,' the wife explained.

" 'That's no kind of love for a child,' the sultan muttered.

"The third wife, whose children were sullen, was harsh and vengeful. When one of her children misbehaved, she punished him severely and repeatedly. 'I love my children so much that I won't allow them to step out of line even a little bit.'

" 'But when do they feel your affection?' the sultan asked.

"The wife scoffed. 'Affection will spoil them!'

"The sultan returned to his first palace, where the children were happy and usually well behaved. When they misbehaved, the mother reprimanded them sternly but not harshly. Then, after she was certain they understood they must not do it again, she pulled them close and loved them.

" 'My children feel my love in two ways,' the wife explained to the sultan. 'First, when I care enough to correct their wrongdoings; second, when I care enough to love them for who they are inside.'

"The sultan was pleased, and he called his other two wives before him. 'Is there joy in your homes?' he asked. 'Do your children bring you happiness from day to day?'

" 'Only sometimes,' the wives admitted. They hung their heads to reflect the disappointment their children brought them.

" 'Here, then, is the solution,' he said 'You both love
your children. You say it, and I know it is true. But if you
wish to have joy with them, love them in two ways. Love
them enough to expect obedience and respect from them,
and love them enough to hold them close after you have
corrected them.' "

Mary put her other arm around John and pulled him
close.

"So what happened?" John asked.

"The other two wives took his counsel to heart. They
saw improvement in their children almost immediately. And
after years of effort and practice and trying to grow and perfect themselves they all lived happily ever after."

She laughed, then added, "I believe we're able to love
our children in that way when we have a true perspective of
who they really are. That's when we're able to treat them
the way the Lord would—correcting their misbehaviors,
then filling them up with love afterwards."

Later that day John smiled when he saw a new sign
stuck on the refrigerator door:

> ***A key to harmony in the home:***
> ***At crisis points***
> ***remember who each person is—***
> ***a beloved child of God***
> ***with eternal possibilities—***
> ***and act accordingly.***

Before he went to bed that night, he took a few minutes
and wrote down what he and Mary had learned about using
the One Minute Secret to help them as parents and as eternal
companions:

Applying the One Minute Secret to the Family —A Summary

1. Building my relationship with my family is one of my most important priorities. I will not allow things that are less important from an eternal perspective to preempt the time and effort I should spend with my family.
2. I will remember that my relationship with my wife must come first, and I will act accordingly.
3. I can show my wife and children how important they are to me by taking a minute every day to give each one a hug and say "I love you."
4. I can build my relationship with my wife and children by spending time with each one every day. I will give them my undivided attention. Since it's hard to find big blocks of time, I will start with one minute, just to get going. Then I will listen with my heart and take it from there.
5. At crisis points in the family, I will take a minute to regain my perspective. I will remember that the other person (my wife or child) is a beloved child of God with eternal possibilities. I will pray for help to live up to what I know about who that person really is. Then I will follow through on what I feel in the prayer.
6. I will love my children in two ways: enough to correct their mistakes and expect obedience and respect, and enough to pull them close after I've reprimanded or punished them.

What Would Jesus Do?

The months passed. John faithfully applied the One Minute Secret to his personal growth and to family concerns. Sometimes he slipped and forgot his new goals—and he often suffered inside for the lapse. Sometimes he was just too tired or too preoccupied to be effective in doing what he wanted to do. But overall he succeeded in his effort.

The results were tangible. He felt more at peace with himself than he could remember ever having been before. He felt closer to his Father in Heaven. His prayers were more meaningful. His study of the scriptures brought greater blessings into his life.

His family life was also much improved. He knew that
he and Mary were falling more in love with each other all the
time. And his children seemed happier and more secure. His
relationship with each member of the family had been
measurably strengthened.

One night Matt Holden stopped by. He held a briefcase
with one hand. "I've been thinking about you quite a bit in
the past few weeks," Matt said. "I've been wanting to see
how things are turning out for you."

John smiled. "Well, Matt, I believe I can say things are
going fairly well since we last talked."

"I believe I can agree with that," Matt said. "I can see in
your countenance that you've made some real progress."

"Thank you," John said. "It's amazing the difference I
feel in my life. Several months ago I felt stagnant and spiritually in limbo. I wasn't committing any great sins, but I
wasn't growing much either. But I don't need to rehearse all
that with you. You already know it."

"I remember how you felt when we first visited. Several
times since then I've wanted to ask how you were feeling
now. But I always decided to let it ride for a while longer."
He stopped speaking and looked around the room. "Can we
sit down for a moment? Or is this a bad time?"

"No, it's a fine time," John said. "Come sit over here."
He gestured toward two rocking chairs that were facing the
fireplace.

Matt sat across from John and looked into the fire.
"What have you learned in these past weeks and months?"
Matt asked.

John was delighted to be able to share his newfound insights. He told Matt about the One Minute Secret, then he
added, "Of course, you already know all about this." He
described the different ways he'd been applying the
secret—with his prayers, with the reading of scriptures,

with family concerns. He told of the new joy that had come into his life. "I feel closer to the Lord than I ever have in my life. And all it took was concentration and a little extra effort."

He paused. Matt did not interrupt.

"Even with all that, I'm still far from perfect," John laughed. "So far, in fact, that I hardly need to even mention it."

Matt rocked for a moment without answering. His face looked thoughtful. Then he stopped, leaned forward, and looked closely at John. "I'm glad to hear you say that. Sometimes when we begin to make progress we become complacent and feel that's all we need to do.

"But the Lord requires us to give him our heart and whole soul, with all our sins. He has asked us to serve him with all our 'heart, might, mind, and strength.'

"When we feel that we've 'arrived,' that we've reached the point where we don't need to seek further improvements in our lives, I'm afraid a sort of pride sets in. Then, instead of growing and progressing, we start to slide backwards.

"The scary part of all this is that, in our feelings of self-satisfaction and self-complacency, we don't even see what we've done to ourselves."

"I don't think you need to worry about me there, Matt," John said. "I can see too many areas of my life that still need some serious work."

Matt nodded. "Me, too, I'm afraid." He started rocking again. "But we should never get discouraged when we see how far we have to go. To paraphrase what one of our latter-day Apostles once said, 'Some people worry overmuch about how fast they are improving their lives. They may be asking the wrong question. Instead of troubling themselves so much about speed, they should ask:

" 'First, am I on the right path?

" 'Second, am I traveling forward, rather than going backward or standing still?'

"I think that perspective is essential. Forward movement is a must, but direction is more important than velocity.

"So, John, you've put your feet on the right path, and you're traveling forward. You even have a plan for progressing on a day-to-day basis. That's more than a lot of us have."

"Well, I am trying," John said.

"That's half the battle," Matt said. "We need to try and we need to try in a way that will really make a difference." He paused, then said, "Not long ago I learned another application of the One Minute Secret that's really helping me in my life. Would you like to hear it?"

"I would," John answered. "I'm ready and eager. A few months ago I would have said I didn't have time to do some of the things I knew I should. Now I know all I need to find is one honest minute. If I will do that, then listen to the whisperings in my heart, I'll get the blessing I'm seeking. The whisperings may tell me to take another minute, or ten minutes, or an hour. And I'm happy to use that time, because I have the inward assurance that I've got my priorities right, that I'm doing the best thing possible during that time.

"Of course, some days I spend a minute or two and no more. But that's so much better than I used to do.

"What I'm saying, Matt, is that I'm deeply grateful for what's happened in my life. I'd love to hear any other ideas that would help me to grow even more."

Matt smiled. "I knew that's how you'd feel." He reached into his briefcase and pulled out a book. He held it up so John could see the front cover. It said *Come Unto Christ,* by Ezra Taft Benson.

"This is a wonderful book," Matt said. "It has given me some great insights and motivation and has strengthened my testimony.

"In chapter 6 President Benson talks about another book, *In His Steps,* by Charles Sheldon. The subtitle of the Sheldon book is *What Would Jesus Do?*" Matt reached into his case and pulled out a copy of *In His Steps.* He showed it to John. "Let me tell you about this book.

"Sheldon was a Protestant minister in Kansas around the turn of the century. He became alarmed at his shrinking congregation, particularly among the youth, and he decided to write a novel to try to motivate people to recommit their lives.

"The novel told about a small group of people who decided to live for an entire year as Jesus would live if he were in their circumstances. Living up to that decision was not easy for the characters in the book, but, as you would suppose, their spiritual rewards were truly great."

John was standing beside the fireplace, watching the dancing flames. "I've heard of that book," he said. "Wasn't it a huge bestseller for the time?"

"For any time," Matt said. "Exact figures aren't available because so many editions have been released by so many publishers, but estimates place total sales at twenty million or more. It's got to be one of the biggest selling books of all time.

"In his book, President Benson quotes part of a *New Era* article by President Marion G. Romney. Apparently President Romney read the Sheldon book when he was a teenager, and it had a powerful effect on him."

Matt flipped through the pages of *Come Unto Christ* until he found the spot he wanted. "Here's what President Romney said:

" 'Countless times as I have faced challenges and vexing decisions I have asked myself "What would Jesus do?" Fortunately, I was exposed early in life to the standard works of the Church. . . . It was therefore natural for me, as I pondered the question, "What would Jesus do?" to turn to the scriptures in search of the answer. . . .

" 'Relying upon the . . . scriptures, I decided in my youth that for me the best approach to the solution of problems and the resolving of questions would be to proceed as Jesus proceeded: foster an earnest desire to do the Lord's will; familiarize myself with what the Lord has revealed on the matter involved; pray with diligence and faith for an inspired understanding of his will and the courage to do it.' "

Matt glanced up at John. John shifted at his post beside the fire.

"After quoting President Romney, President Benson concludes with these words," Matt said. " 'There is no greater . . . challenge than to try to learn of Christ and walk in His steps. . . . "What would Jesus do?" or "What would He have me do?" are the paramount personal questions of this life. Walking in His way is the greatest achievement of life.' "

He closed the book and put it down. He spoke in a quiet voice. "I've tried this. It is not easy. Sometimes I forget to even think about it. But, all in all, it has had a profound effect on my life."

John didn't answer. He was thinking about what Matt had said.

"Here's what I do," Matt continued. "As I go through each day, I try to be aware of the decisions I make. Most of them I can make on my own, using my experience and common sense to help me.

"But sometimes I have to make a decision that could really matter. For example, one of my children misbehaves. What should I do? Or I'm blessed with a few minutes of spare time. How should I spend it? Or something happens that makes me angry. How should I handle it? Maybe I'm faced with one of life's little dilemmas. Which direction should I go? Or life is demanding more of me than I feel I can handle. What should I do to deal with it? Or I'm reminded of a duty to God or my fellowmen that I'm not fulfilling as well as I should. How should I react?

"There are dozens of these decisions we make every week. We can usually choose between several options. Often we make the decision by habit, without even thinking about it.

"But now I know a better way. Choose as Jesus would choose. Do what he would do."

John moved away from the fire and sat on the raised hearth, directly in front of Matt. "I know what you're saying." His voice was animated. "Before we act on important things in our lives, we should stop, take one minute, and begin the process of thinking through what Jesus would do in the same situation."

"That's right," Matt said. "And it's not as hard to decide on that basis as we might think. When we combine our basic gospel understanding with the words of the scriptures, then add the promptings of the Spirit, we can know with some certainty what the Savior would do."

"I see how this really will help me draw closer to the Lord," John said. "And it will help me to reach my ultimate goal—to become like him."

He pulled his notebook from his pocket. "Excuse me while I write this down." He found a blank page and wrote:

Applying the One Minute Secret to Decisions and Actions—A Summary

1. When I am faced with an important decision or action, I will stop and consider the problem from a gospel perspective.
2. I will ask, "What would Jesus do?"
3. I will decide the answer to that question based on my gospel understanding, the scriptures, and the Spirit.
4. I will do it!

"I like what you've put there," Matt said. "Of course, the *doing* is often the hardest part. You may find that you don't like the answer you come up with by following that process. I know that's happened to me more often than I care to admit. I've discovered that doing things the way the Lord would do them is not often the easiest way."

"I have a friend who likes to talk about that," John said. "He has a motto that I have tried to apply to my own life." He opened his notebook again, turned a few pages, and read:

It is seldom convenient to do the right thing.

"Yes," Matt said. "But we need to make a commitment that we'll do it anyway. In fact, if we've been baptized we've already made such a commitment. Maybe we should think a little more about what we sing in the popular gospel song." And he repeated the words:

**Do what is right;
Let the consequence follow.**

John repeated the words thoughtfully, then said, "We come back to the point where we started. If we will only be conscious of where we're going in our lives, then take a minute at critical times to step onto the right path, we'll find ourselves gradually becoming all that we had hoped."

"And all that our Father intended," Matt added softly.

Sharing the Gift

As the years passed, both John and Mary struggled to apply the ideas they'd learned. Some weeks and months they slipped back into their old habits, hardly thinking of the One Minute Secret. Other times they focused their thinking and their desires and found increasing joy in their lives as they made efforts to grow in their obedience and spirituality.

John was encouraged to discover that the farther he progressed along the right path, the more motivated he was to continue.

"Maybe I should compare it to climbing a mountain," he said to Mary one day. "The higher up the mountain slope I get, the greater the vistas that come into view. And when I look back and see how far I've come, little step by little step, my heart swells with gratitude for the marvelous help I've received on my journey. Not far ahead lies the mountain peak. It becomes much easier to continue upward than to go back."

Mary nodded and took his hand. "I had a religion professor at BYU who said there are three kinds of people who get onto the strait and narrow path.

"First are those who aren't really committed to the gospel. They soon turn off the path and wander in broad ways and are lost.

"Second are those who like the path and what it has to offer. But they don't want to make the effort to progress. They set up tents on the side of the path and watch the others trek past.

"Third are those whose hearts are burning with testimony and desire to do right. They take their staves in hand and climb onward and upward."

John squeezed her hand. "If we rest on our laurels they'll wilt," he said. "I'm sure grateful you want to climb with me."

Both John and Mary served in many positions in the Church as the years marched by. More than once they were approached by people who had become acquainted with them. "I hope you don't feel I'm being too personal," the other person would say, "but you have a radiance about you. You seem happy. You seem secure in the course you've chosen in life. What can I do to find the joy you've found?"

One day John was visiting one of the families he'd been assigned as a home teacher. The man of the house, David, came to the door. "I know I've already been by once this month," John said. "But I was driving past and thought I'd stop and say hello."

"I'm glad you did," David said. "In fact, I've been wanting to talk to you. Come on in and make yourself comfortable."

John sat on the couch. David sat in an overstuffed chair facing him. "In all my years in the Church," David began, "I don't think I've ever had a home teacher who cared for me as much as you do."

"I'm thankful for the opportunity to serve you and your family," John said.

"Tell me your secret, John," David said. "What do you do to make the gospel so vital in your life?"

"It's no secret. Long ago a friend taught me a simple couplet." He spoke the words slowly and deliberately:

To know the Lord, here is the way:
Study, pray, serve, and obey.

"That puts it into a nutshell, doesn't it," David said.

"It does," John said. "In other words, there is no secret to living the gospel. All we need to do is follow what we've been taught over and over and over again."

He paused. "There is a kind of secret I can tell you, though. It's a little mechanism some friends helped me discover many years ago. It won't give you any shortcuts to the celestial kingdom. But it will help you get your mind in gear so you can more effectively focus your thoughts and efforts. It will help you pay attention to things that are important but sometimes forgotten.

"We call it the One Minute Secret.

"There's nothing mysterious about it. It's just an approach to time that helps me to do the things the Lord wants me to do. In fact, all it does is carve my time into small enough pieces that I can really concentrate on doing the things the scriptures tell me to do."

John told David the story about how he had gone on his own search for a way to build his spirituality. "I was doing most of the things the prophets tell us to do. What I discovered, though, was that I wasn't doing them consistently enough—or thoughtfully enough.

"I was praying every day, but almost by rote. I wasn't really praying from my heart.

"I was reading the scriptures almost every day. But there were plenty of days when I didn't get around to it. And when I did read I rushed through the verses without giving them a whole lot of thought."

"I'm afraid I'm guilty of that, too," David said. "I feel I'm in a rut, but I'm not sure how to build the momentum to get myself out."

"That's how I was. Then I found out about the One Minute Secret and everything changed for me. It gave me some powerful forward inertia and helped me to move ahead with new commitment.''

John reached into his coat pocket and pulled out a notebook. He opened it to the first page. ''Here's what I'm talking about. Read this and it will outline what I've done that's been so helpful.''

He handed the notebook to David. David leaned his head over the page and read:

Applying the One Minute Secret to My Life— A Summary

1. A minute has power. I will remember that if I can make my key minutes count, my life will take care of itself. Small efforts, done often, can bring to pass big results.
2. I will use a key minute to prepare myself before I pray. Even a minute's thought and preparation will strengthen my communication.
3. I will listen to the Spirit as I pray. Then, after my prayer, I will use a key minute to write down what I learned from the prayer. I will write down what I'm going to do.
4. I will use a key minute when I read the scriptures each day. I will take at least one minute to ponder what I've read. I will write down new insights and things I need to do.
5. I will use a key minute with my wife and with each of my children every day. I will take a minute and give each one a hug and say, "I love you." Then I will give each one my undivided attention during another key minute each day. After the first minute, I will spend additional time with each one as my heart tells me to do.
6. When crisis erupts in my home, I will use a key minute to regain my perspective. Before I react with hasty solutions, I will take at least one minute to remember that my wife and children are beloved children of God with eternal possibilities. I will particularly think of the person who is giving me trouble at the moment. I will pray for help to live up to what I know. Then I will do it.

7. When I am met with challenges and problems and decisions each day, I will use a key minute to ensure that I will reach the proper solution. I will stop and consider the problem for at least one minute, asking "What would Jesus do?" Then I will make my decision based on my gospel understanding, the scriptures, and the promptings of the Spirit.

David looked up from the paper. "Does this really work? It seems so simple."

"Maybe that's why it works," John said. He was smiling. "After all, if it's simple, maybe you'll be inclined to try it. And when you find out it works, you'll want to continue with it."

"I can see that it would focus my thinking and my efforts better than I've been doing."

"Exactly. And that focus is a key to your success. Getting focused is like having your eye single to the spiritual things you need to accomplish each day. And if your eye is single to God's glory, the scriptures say, your whole body shall be filled with light. What a blessing!"

"Yes, that would be a blessing," David said quietly.

"One other thing I hope you'll keep in mind," John said. "Remember this: *You will generally grow only as much as you exert a conscious effort to make the gospel active in your life.*"

"So why don't more of us *consciously* pursue greater excellence in our lives?"

"That's one of the great paradoxes of life. The answer is that we just don't think to do it!"

John stood, reached over, and rested his hand on David's shoulder. "Will you keep me posted?" he asked.

David nodded. "I would like it if we could talk about this some more when you come on your visits."

"I would be delighted."

John put his notebook back into his pocket and turned to leave. David followed him to the door. But John stopped before he pulled it open. "David, does the Lord want you to succeed in your efforts to draw closer to him?"

"Of course," David answered. "That's one of the main reasons he's given us the gospel plan, with the Church, the prophets, spiritual support, and everything else."

"Has he commanded you to draw closer to him?"

"Yes, he has. Some of the scriptures tell us to do exactly that."

"I agree," John said. "And with that in mind, remember that our Heavenly Father is prepared to support you and help you in your efforts. When things seem to get difficult, when trials rear their ugly heads, when you wonder if you'll ever become all you want to, remember that we've been *commanded* to progress. And remember Nephi's promise to us all." John then repeated the promise in his own words:

*The Lord will never give us a commandment
without providing a way for us to obey it.*

John turned and faced David squarely. "When you get discouraged or frustrated, remember that you're not alone in this," he said.

"You've got a partner—the most powerful and most loving being in the universe.

"And he wants you to succeed."